Brothers

Brothers

An Inside Look

Larry Schatz, FSC

Saint Mary's Press
Christian Brothers Publications
Winona, Minnesota

Genuine recycled paper with 10% post-consumer waste.
Printed with soy-based ink.

The publishing team included Shirley Kelter, development editor; Paul Grass, FSC, copy editor; Brooke Saron, production editor; Laurie Geisler, art director; cover and inside image by Digital Imagery copyright © 2001 PhotoDisc, Inc.; manufactured by the production services department of Saint Mary's Press.

The acknowledgments continue on page 66.

Printed in the United States of America

Printing: 9 8 7 6 5 4 3 2 1

Year: 2010 09 08 07 06 05 04 03 02

ISBN 0-88489-721-4

Library of Congress Cataloging-in-Publication Data

Schatz, Larry.
    Brothers: an inside look / Larry Schatz.
        p. cm.
Includes bibliographical references (p. 65).
ISBN 0-88489-721-4
    1. Brothers (Religious) 2. Vocations (in religious orders, congregations, etc.) 3. Schatz, Larry. I. Title.
BX2835 .S35 2002
255'.092—dc21
                                                                2001005715

This book is dedicated to my loving parents,
Clemence and Minnie Schatz,
who have shown me what it means
to live a committed life.

Contents

Series Foreword

An old Hasidic legend about the mysterious nature of life says that God whispers into your newly created soul all the secrets of your existence, all the divine love for you, and your unique purpose in life. Then, just as God infuses your soul into your body, an assisting angel presses your mouth shut and instructs your soul to forget its preternatural life.

You are now spending your time on earth seeking to know once again the God who created you, loves you, and assigns you a singular purpose. Raise your forefinger to feel the crease mark the angel left above your lips, and ask yourself in wonder: Who am I? How am I uniquely called to live in the world?

The authors of the five titles in this Vocations series tell how they approached these same questions as they searched for meaning and purpose in their Christian vocation, whether as a brother, a married couple, a priest, a single person, or a sister.

Christians believe that God creates a dream for each person. What is your dream in life? This is how Pope John Paul II, echoing Jeremiah 1:5, speaks of the Creator's dream and the divine origin of your vocation:

> All human beings, from their mothers' womb, belong to God who searches them and knows them, who forms them and knits them together with his own hands, who gazes on them when they are tiny shapeless embryos

and already sees in them the adults of tomorrow whose days are numbered and whose vocation is even now written in the "book of life." (*Evangelium Vitae,* no. 61)

In spite of believing that God does have your specific vocation in mind, you probably share the common human experience—the tension and the mystery—of finding out who you are and how God is personally calling you to live in this world. Although you can quickly recognize the uniqueness of your thumbprint, you will spend a lifetime deciphering the full meaning of your originality.

There is no shortage of psychological questionnaires for identifying your personality type, career path, learning style, and even a compatible mate. Although these methods can be helpful in your journey to self-discovery, they do little to illuminate the mystery in your quest. What is the best approach to knowing your vocation in life? Follow the pathway as it unfolds before you and live with the questions that arise along the way.

The stories in this Vocations series tell about life on the path of discernment and choice; they remind you that you are not alone. God is your most present and patient companion. In the "travelogues" of these authors, you will find reassurance that even when you relegate the Divine Guide to keeping ten paces behind you, or when you abandon the path entirely for a time, you cannot undo God's faithfulness to you. Each vocation story uniquely testifies to the truth that God is always at work revealing your life's purpose to you.

In these stories you will also find that other traveling companions— family, friends, and classmates—contribute to your discovery of a place in the world and call forth the person you are becoming. Their companionship along the way not only manifests God's abiding presence but reminds you to respect others for their gifts, which highlight and mirror your own.

Although each path in the Vocations series is as unique as the person who tells his or her story, these accounts remind you to be patient with the mystery of your own life, to have confidence in God's direction, and to listen to the people and events you encounter as you journey to discover your unique role in God's plan. By following your path, you too will come to see the person of tomorrow who lives in you today.

Clare vanBrandwijk

Introduction

20 January 2001

In today's mail I received a letter from one of my brothers who has just completed a prayer workshop at the Sangre de Cristo Retreat Center in New Mexico. He is in temporary vows—a required time of living religious life before taking final vows—and has been discerning his vocation to religious life. In a beautifully written letter that reflects a sense of peace and resolution, he states that although he has great respect and love for the brothers, he has decided not to renew his vows.

Before I started reading the letter, in my heart I already knew what it would say, but I still hoped that perhaps this young man was going to tell me that he had resolved to take final vows. It is always bittersweet news to get word that someone is leaving the brothers. On the one hand, I am happy that the man departing has a sense of peace and knows that he is being called elsewhere. On the other hand, I am sad and disappointed to lose a family member, for this is what the brothers are in my life—a vast family. I am linked with them not by blood but rather by a common vision and dream. It is hard for me to see someone leave.

A letter like the one I received today forces me once again to examine my commitment to this rather unusual life. There is a lot of mystery to this thing called "a religious vocation," but one fact I do know. Br. Brian Henderson, FSC, said it so simply a few years ago while sharing his life story with me: "Brotherhood is my way to God." I realized that in these six words he had captured why I am a brother. I hope to share with you the journey of my life as a brother and why this vocation is my way to God.

I should note here that the letters *FSC* after Brian's name and mine signify the Latin words *Fratres Scholarum Christianarum*, "Brothers of the Christian Schools," the official name of the religious institute to which he and I belong. Also known as De La Salle Brothers and in the United States of America as Christian Brothers, the Institute of the Brothers of the Christian Schools was founded by Saint John Baptist de La Salle in France over three hundred years ago. People often use the word *Lasallian*, derived from the founder's name, to describe the mission, the identity, and the people who share the brothers' educational ministry. Even though I am writing about my life as a De La Salle Christian Brother, much of what I say about my vocation pertains to all brothers in the church. So, here is my story. . . .

The Call

The Brochure

It all started with a brochure. I was teaching at a girls' academy in southern Minnesota; while monitoring a study hall one afternoon, I opened my desk drawer to look for a pen and ran across a brochure I had placed there several weeks before. A vocation awareness day for all Catholic youth had taken place at the school, and representatives from several religious orders were present. Someone from the De La Salle Christian Brothers had used my classroom and left some brochures on my desk. I remember wondering why he had done so in a girls' school, not a likely source of vocations for brothers!

I picked up the brochure and casually paged through it. I remember being attracted by the cover, an image of a man paddling a canoe, and by the words, "If one is a Christian, there is a point. . . ." I was curious: what is the *point?*

The point is that there comes a time when you need to commit to living the Christian life fully. The brochure talked about the Christian Brothers, about living in community, about teaching, about faith. I liked what I read.

In my third year of teaching, I was feeling a nudge to move on and make a change. For the past few months, my final prayer before I crawled into bed at night had been, "God, if there's something you want me to do, let me know." I guess that is all God needed to hear because suddenly and rather surprisingly, this brochure spoke to me about things I knew I wanted. I wanted to teach in Catholic schools, and after three years of living alone, I knew I needed others in my life. I was struck by the emphasis on community and the shared life. It was time to start paddling my canoe in a different direction.

"God, if there's something you want me to do, let me know."

So, I wrote a letter to the vocation director of the Christian Brothers and asked for more information. I expected to receive a packet in the mail, but what I got instead was much better. One of the brothers called me to ask if he could drive over from Winona and meet me. We could go out to dinner and talk. It sounded good to me!

So began my encounter with a group of men I would come to know very well. Br. Tom Sullivan met me at school, and we had a good long visit. What it came down to was this: because I was already a certified high school teacher, if I was interested in finding out more about the De La Salle Brothers, I could enter the brother candidate program and live in community with them while teaching in a Lasallian school. He assured me that this would not involve any heavy commitment on my part, but it would be a realistic way of experiencing what life is like as a brother.

He also mentioned that a candidate retreat was coming up that I could attend to meet some more brothers and spend time with other guys in my same position. What impressed me the most was that Brother Tom was so friendly and down to earth. Like many other people, I had the tendency to put brothers, sisters, and priests on a pedestal. It was clear to me that Brother Tom had no desire to be atop a pedestal. Neither did I!

An adventure began that winter evening that continues to this day. Opening their brochure and sharing a meal with one of the brothers led to a fulfilling life full of surprises.

Moving On

By late spring I had secured a teaching job in one of the Lasallian high schools and had decided to live in community with the brothers as a brother candidate. This stage of formation, or preparation for religious life, has several different names depending on the specific congregation and locale. Some orders call this phase the postulancy or the pre-novitiate. I like the name *candidate* because that is what I was, and the term seemed clear to me. I had decided to give the brother's life a try for at least a year. I was assured that if I changed my mind, I would still have a teaching job, so it seemed to me that I couldn't lose.

Of course, now the challenge would be what to tell everyone about what I was doing. After all, my decision sort of came out of the blue, and I wasn't sure what this experience was all about. I just knew I had to give it a try.

I had gone home for Easter, which is when I told my parents about my plans. I couldn't quite tell what their rather neutral reaction signified. They certainly knew what a religious vocation is. My mom's two youngest sisters, as well as three of her cousins, are Benedictine sisters. Because I grew up near a Benedictine abbey, my family knew several of the monks, both brothers and priests. One of my dad's relatives was a brother at that abbey.

Later, I discovered the reason for their rather reserved reaction. The only brothers my mom and dad knew were the brothers from the abbey, and when my parents were growing up in the era before Vatican Council II, the brothers tended to be the manual laborers in the abbey. They generally were the ones who tended the farm and the grounds, and they took care of all the other tasks that kept the abbey going. The priests were the teachers and pastors; they had the college degrees.

What confused my parents is why I would want to become a brother when I was already a college graduate and a teacher. This reaction became clear to me only after they visited my community that fall and realized that the institute I was interested in is a congregation of brothers who are educators. Once that became clear to them, they understood the step I had taken and became very supportive.

Brothers now take on a variety of roles.

I do want to emphasize that things have changed a lot for all brothers, especially those in a monastic community. Brothers now take on a variety of roles in a monastery; many of them are teachers and administrators. For example, at Saint John's Abbey in Collegeville, Minnesota, where I did my undergraduate study, a brother currently serves as president of Saint John's University. This appointment might not have happened in times past.

Telling my friends what I was planning to do was more difficult because I wasn't completely sure how they'd react. What I usually told them was that I got a job in a Christian Brothers' school and that I planned to live with the brothers "just to try it out." I generally ended the explanation by saying, "but I'm not sure it will work out." This comment seemed to reassure my friends that I wasn't doing anything rash, but it also gave me an out. However, I had a strong feeling inside that this decision might work out better than I was letting on. I liked what I had seen during my weekend visit with the brothers in Stevens Point, Wisconsin, where I would be living and teaching.

Toward the end of summer, I left the life I knew in Mankato, Minnesota, loaded up a truck with my stuff, and headed to central Wisconsin. I wasn't sure what lay ahead, but I was excited about the change, and I was certainly willing to give this "brother thing" an honest try.

What's in a Name?

Because I had been teaching for three years, I was used to being called Mr. Schatz. The name was hard to accept at first because it seemed so formal; I felt it was more properly my dad's name than mine. Now the brothers gave me the option of being called Brother Larry. Typically, a brother candidate has the choice whether to use the title Brother.

I hesitated at first, but the brother director of the community suggested that I give it a try. He gave me a few rather convincing reasons. The main one was that it would be simpler all around because I was living with the brothers in community, I was new at the school, and the name would help me get a clearer idea of how it felt to be a brother. I wouldn't recommend this step for everyone; I think your decision will depend on where you are in your process of discernment. The choice of the title *Brother* made sense to me at the time because I was new to the school and would be identified with the brothers.

So it came to be. I was Brother Larry, a name that to me is now so familiar and important that I hardly recall anymore what it was like being Mr. Schatz. But at first when I would hear the word *Brother*, it would take me a moment to realize that I was being addressed. Students must have wondered about my delayed reaction; however, it didn't take me long to adjust to the name.

I noticed one thing: although I was comfortable with that name in my new school and community, everywhere else I was still just Larry. I almost felt at times as if I had two identities: I was Brother Larry in one part of my life and Larry Schatz in the other. It took some time for the two to meld into one. Looking back, I have no regrets about adopting the title of Brother when I did; the name helped me better understand what being a brother is all about.

I quickly grew to cherish the title of Brother. What I like is that the name implies a unique and special relationship that is very different from Father, for example. Having a big brother and having a dad are two distinct realities. Although I do not have an older brother, I do understand what it means to be a brother to my two sisters.

I also understand and appreciate now what it means to be a brother to my students. I am not in a parental role so much as in a fraternal one. I am called to be a big brother to the students I serve. I like what this relationship implies. A big brother is someone who looks out for you, cares about what happens to you, and can be both a mentor and a buddy. Every now and then, someone will address me as Father Larry, an honest mistake because the title of Father in Catholic circles is much more common than Brother. I always gently correct the person who has spoken. It is important for people to know that I am a brother and not a priest; the two roles are quite different. (I will speak more about the difference later on.)

Brother is far more than a title.

The identity of brother and the relationship it implies, particularly with young people, are very rich. *Brother* is far more than a title; it challenges me to be in relationship with others and not to take the relationship for granted. As someone once said rather cleverly, "You cannot spell *brothers* without spelling *others*." I like that!

My New Life

So, how was my life different now that I was living in a brothers' community? There were two big changes, for sure. I prayed more, and I spent a lot more time at the dinner table. There were eight of us in the community that first year. All were involved at Pacelli High School, which the De La Salle Christian Brothers had staffed since its beginning in the mid-1950s. I was a full-time English teacher with the extra responsibilities of moderating the school paper and developing a debating and public-speaking program.

Because of our different morning schedules, the community chose to pray together in the late afternoon, before dinner. My congregation requires every community to gather at the beginning of the school year to determine its Community Annual Program, or CAP as we call it. The meeting is important because the community establishes the daily rhythm as well as everything else: from discussing the annual budget to figuring out who will take care of the various household tasks. One key decision is what prayer time will work for everyone.

One key decision is what prayer time will work for everyone.

Herein lies a distinctive difference between what are called *monastic* and *apostolic* religious communities. In a monastery such as Saint John's, a Benedictine community, the prayer times are set. The rest of the day revolves around them. A contemplative congregation such as the Trappists gathers for prayer five or six times throughout the day, from early morning to early evening. Prayer and silence are the primary features of their day.

In an apostolic congregation of brothers whose focus is a ministry of education or health care, the prayer times need to be determined by the necessities of the daily schedule of professional work. Typically, in an apostolic community, especially one with education as its primary mission, the brothers gather for prayer in the morning and in the late afternoon or early evening.

Whenever possible, brothers participate daily in the eucharistic celebration. In times past, when priests were more abundant, some large communities would have a chaplain in residence. A priest would live in the community house with the brothers and be available to celebrate the Eucharist daily. Today, such a situation is rare; the brothers generally go to a local parish for the eucharistic celebration or invite a priest to their community once a week. The demands of the school schedule some-times make it impossible for the brothers to attend Mass every day.

Although the institute to which I belong, the De La Salle Christian Brothers, consists only of brothers, some men's congregations in the Catholic church have both brothers and priests as members; one or more priests are often part of their local community. I will speak more about this point later because the many different orders and customs in reli-gious life may seem confusing to you.

How do brothers pray together?

How do brothers pray together? There are several options. The most familiar and commonly used form of prayer is the Liturgy of the Hours. This set of prayers, drawn mainly from the Book of Psalms in the Bible, is a four-week cycle of prayers based on the liturgical seasons of the church. Prayers, psalms, and other selections from the Scriptures are read or chanted in two alternating choirs, or groups. These prayers and read-ings are also called the Prayer of Christians, a traditional prayer form available to all believers.

Generally, the prayer leader in a community will alternate weekly and is free to design the format of the prayer. Whatever form it takes, community prayer includes the Scriptures, music, and an opportunity for shared prayer.

The format of the prayer is not as important as the fact that the brothers gather for prayer. Praying together is an essential support in a brother's life. The prayer may be in a chapel in larger and more traditional communities, in a special prayer room set aside in the brothers' residence, or in the living room of a small community of two or three brothers. The place is not as important as the fact of gathering and praying.

I look forward to times of community prayer because of the great sense of support and peace in knowing that we are centered on God together. Christian Brothers around the world all begin prayer with the same invitation in whatever language they speak: "Let us remember that we are in the holy presence of God."

Another highlight of community life for me is having dinner together at the end of the day. After three years of living alone and making my own meals, often eating them while watching television, I enjoyed the treat of gathering around a table with several others and sharing a meal. Often our meals together take an hour or more simply because we are busy conversing and enjoying one another's company. For me it is a sacred time.

Shared meal times . . . are
a vital part of community life.

I am sure that Jesus spent much time at the table sharing meals and conversation with his followers. It is important to remember that Jesus comes to you and me in the form of bread and wine. He nourishes us spiritually with food and drink. Shared meal times, which are becoming rare in busy families and homes, are a vital part of community life and have always been one of my favorite times with the brothers.

Another conclusion that struck me during my first year of living in community is how good it felt to be with others who shared my values, ideals, and profession. Everyone in that community was an educator and a brother united by the vision of Saint John Baptist de La Salle, our Founder. This powerful support system is especially helpful for a new teacher in a school.

In spite of their quirks and idiosyncrasies, I quickly learned to enjoy these men with whom I was living. After all, they had to put up with me as well! Because we varied in age from twenty-one to sixty-three, the community certainly enjoyed a variety of backgrounds and temperaments. All things considered, this was a great place for me to begin my adventure as a brother. I am thankful that God led me to this community and school. I learned much and realized that I was even more content than I had ever thought I would be.

Promises to Keep

What kind of commitment did I make that first year? I was living with the brothers, sharing fully in community life, and yet I had not taken any formal vows to be a brother. I will say more about the vows later on, but I tell you now that clearly there were some expectations placed on me as a brother candidate. I would try to live as much like a "real" brother as possible. In practical terms this commitment meant that I would not date, I would share my earnings with the community, and I would make significant decisions within the context of the men with whom I lived and shared my life. Because only a brother who has completed the novitiate (the stage after candidacy) can profess vows, I was actually making a promise to live the vows as fully as possible but without any legal requirement to do so in the eyes of the church.

In early October of that first year, we had a special Mass at our house during which I made promises to my community to live the vows as best I could for one year as a brother candidate. I invited my parents down for the weekend to be present to witness my promises and to meet the brothers of my community. This visit is when they realized that the Christian Brothers are different than the brothers they had known in the past. Because all the brothers are educators, it made perfect sense to them that I was considering becoming part of this group. My parents felt very much at home with the brothers.

When people visit a brothers' community,
they feel welcome.

I often hear this same comment: when people visit a brothers' community, they feel welcome. Visitors immediately notice the spirit of hospitality, perhaps because they never know quite what to expect in a "religious" house, and they enter with more than a few apprehensions. In times past, religious houses were generally off limits to outsiders. Family members were welcomed in a front parlor or visiting room, but the rest of the house was a cloister, closed to all but community members.

Because the De La Salle Christian Brothers belong to an international institute, they have community residences in eighty countries around the world. I have visited a few brothers' houses outside the United States, mainly in Europe and Mexico, and I have always felt welcome. My friends often say to me, "Join the brothers, and see the world." Well, there is some truth to that comment. It's nice to know I have a family and a place to stay all over the world.

Now I had promised to try to live the life of a brother for one year and see how it fit. So far, it fit just fine!

Chapter 2

The Novitiate and First Vows

A Time Apart

The next two years seemed to fly by. I was now a seasoned teacher and had found my stride in the classroom. I thoroughly enjoyed teaching and the extracurricular activities in which I was involved. I felt more and more at home with the brothers. Looming on the horizon, however, was the next step, the novitiate. The church's legislation (*Code of Canon Law*) requires every individual contemplating religious life to make a novitiate. Some congregations require one year and some two, but the minimum time is twelve months (canon 648).

What is a novitiate? Where does this strange term come from? The Latin word *nova* means "new." Someone making a novitiate is called a novice, a "new one." Novitiate year is unlike any other experience. The focus is on prayer, personal and spiritual growth, learning more about religious life and the vows, and especially spending lots of time discerning.

Discerning is a great word for the process of figuring out where to go and what to do next, but the context is spiritual. For instance, you *decide* where you are going Friday night and what you will do, but you *discern* where God is calling you and in what type of ministry you can best serve God. Both situations involve decisions, but discernment implies a much more profound process and significance.

I remember well that one of the brothers talked with me about the novitiate and told me that I had better start preparing for it because I was going to have a lot of "down time." In other words, there would be lots of free time and an expectation that I would spend much of it praying and thinking. I have to admit that because I am an extrovert, this was a rather daunting prospect.

You discern *where God is calling you.*

I get energy from activity and from interaction with others. Being alone does not energize me; besides, I love being active, busy, and involved. During the novitiate I would be parked in one place for a year with no real work to do and in a house where everyone was in the same boat. Looking ahead to this "boat ride" called novitiate filled me with a sense of apprehension. How was this going to work?

I began my novitiate year with five other candidates plus the two brothers on the staff: the director of novices and his assistant. The novitiate that year was located in Windsor, Ontario (across the river from Detroit, Michigan), in a house owned by the Toronto district of the brothers. We novices were from three Midwest districts: Chicago, Saint Louis, and Saint Paul–Minneapolis.

This is probably a good place to talk a bit about how the De La Salle Christian Brothers are organized. The same system would be true for many other apostolic institutes. Unlike the Benedictine monasteries, for instance, which are autonomous—that is, independent from one another —the Institute of the Brothers of the Christian Schools is one large organization divided into districts, or provinces. A provincial (also called Brother Visitor) heads each district.

The Brother Superior General, aided by his council, leads the entire institute and resides at the international headquarters in Rome. The term of the Superior General is seven years and is renewable. One of his duties is to visit every district in the world at least once during his term. Delegates chosen by each district elect the Superior General during an international meeting, a General Chapter, that meets every seven years. The General Chapter acts much like a legislature; it introduces, discusses, and votes on resolutions and elects leaders. The delegates to the General Chapter represent the entire institute and are the highest authority during the several weeks when the General Chapter is in session.

There are currently six districts in the United States of America. Because there are fewer brothers now than in the past, some districts in different parts of the world, particularly those within the same country, have decided to merge to create more efficient and effective government and ministry. In the mid-1990s, for instance, the three districts I mentioned previously combined to form the Midwest District.

So, to return to my story, there we were, all "stuck together" for one year without a lot to do but with plenty of time to do it! Each week we had classes led by a variety of speakers over the course of the year. We prayed and worshiped together at least twice a day. We took turns preparing meals and doing household chores. We had plenty of time to read, go for walks, and think. We went on two extended retreats—one during Holy Week and the other at the end of our novitiate year. We also had several desert days—special times set aside for silence and for reflection on a particular scriptural passage or a selected reading.

All this soul searching is deliberate, of course. Being in an apostolic institute, the brothers lead busy lives, often immersed in classes and after-school activities. They do not have a lot of time to spend reflecting and praying, much as they would like to. This one novitiate year was the time when each novice could catch up with himself. Because we all had taught for at least a year or two and lived in community, we had some lived experience as a brother on which to reflect. In this sense we weren't truly novices, although we were still new to the life of being a brother.

Looking back now, I realize that it certainly was a luxury to have so much time to read, to exercise, and just "to be." At the time we didn't always appreciate the experience, mainly because we lived so closely and intensely. We would get on one another's nerves, much like any family does. Dinner conversation generally didn't revolve around what we had done that day because we knew that already! All in all, the year was a good one, however challenging it could be at times. By the end of the year, one man had left after discerning that being a brother was not the life God is calling him to. The rest of us decided to take the next step, pending the approval of our district, which has the final say about whether a novice will go on to take vows.

Did we pass the novitiate test? Did we have what it takes? Were we truly brother material? I guess we were! The five of us were accepted to take our first vows as brothers. These would be temporary vows, however. We still had a few more years to try this on before we—and the brothers—decided that this vocation was indeed a good fit.

One Year at a Time

Novitiate ended, and five of us went back to our district and to *work*—a word that does not accurately describe what most brothers do. Somehow the term *job* doesn't fit either. No, *ministry* is more like it, or *mission* or *calling*.

Teaching may be my profession, but being a brother is my life. Part of what the novitiate is all about is coming to the realization that the work a brother does is much more than just work. Lots of people claim to hate their job. It is hard to imagine a brother being in this position; as a brother, you live out much of your life involved in serving others, particularly the young. If you decide to become a brother, the challenge will be to love what you do, especially to love those you serve.

Teaching may be my profession, but being a brother is my life.

We graduated novices went back to our district with a deeper sense of what we were about as brothers. I knew that I could never look at teaching the same way again. I now understood that I was called to do so much more than merely teach. I was called to touch the hearts of my students and to inspire them with the Christian spirit, to paraphrase the words of Saint de La Salle.

Touching hearts implies a relationship, it seems to me, that mirrors the kind of effect Jesus must have had on people when he spoke to them. The name that had become so familiar to me—Brother Larry—now called me to a challenging task: I was responsible for the well-being and spiritual growth of each and every one of my students. This would be no small task, I knew, but I wasn't alone. I had the company of plenty of men who shared my vision, and, of course, I had my deepest friend and most ardent supporter in God. This vocation would never be a path I need travel alone.

It wasn't always easy to keep this perspective. Typically, we graduated novices were chomping at the bit to get back into the classroom and live a more normal community life. Each of us made temporary vows. We were brothers faithfully living the vowed life, as it is sometimes called, but the church reasons that we still might need more time before taking the plunge as a "lifer." This made sense. Life after novitiate would definitely have its challenges, and it was a good idea to take a few more years to see if this truly was the life for me.

All religious orders have a period of temporary vows.

Canon law requires at least a three-year period between the end of novitiate and the profession of final vows; six years is the longest a person can wait before making final vows (canon 655). The term for this in-between time, *temporary profession*, means that a person professes vows for one to three years at a time. All religious orders have a period of temporary vows. When a brother decides that he is ready to make a lifetime commitment and the district leadership agrees, he makes a retreat, often called the final vow retreat.

Before a brother professes final vows, all the professed brothers in his district vote on the candidate; everyone has a voice. The candidate must also be approved by the district council and ultimately by the provincial. This sounds like a lot to go through to get the green light, but the regulations make sense when you think about it. You are becoming a lifetime member of a group. You are in essence becoming a full-fledged member of a family. After you live the life for a number of years, go through spiritual boot camp (as the novitiate is sometimes called), and get to know a lot of the brothers, the time comes to say the big yes.

My decision, of course, was never only mine to make. I will live out my life in community, so it stands to reason that the decision for my final vows is as much an *our* decision as a *my* decision.

What does this "yes" involve? A lot of things, certainly, but definitely it includes consenting to live out the three vows common to all religious: poverty, chastity, and obedience. This seems like a good time to take a closer look at the three vows.

Chapter 3

Living the Vows over the Long Haul

The Big Three

Poverty. Chastity. Obedience. There they are: the "big three." According to canon law, every member of a religious order must profess publicly these three vows (canon 654). My congregation, the De La Salle Christian Brothers, requires its members to profess two vows special to the order: to associate for service of poor people through education, and to ensure stability in the institute.

The first special vow calls the brothers to associate and to strive constantly to make their schools and educational works accessible to poor people. This is the work not of a single brother but of a community of brothers and Lasallians who together make this happen. This vow challenges all Lasallians to serve economically disadvantaged people in all schools, including those that enroll students from the middle and upper classes.

The vow of stability reminds the brothers to be faithful to their worldwide institute and to its members and traditions. Stability is a fitting response to the faithfulness of God, who guides the global institute to serve as a stable force in the life of hundreds of thousands of young people.

Other congregations may also have particular vows, but the bottom line for nuns and monks, sisters and brothers, and priests who are members of a religious order (Jesuits, for example, or Dominicans) is the three fundamental vows. *Fundamental* is a good way of describing them because the vows touch almost every meaningful aspect of life.

How is a vow different from a promise? The difference is similar to how discerning differs from deciding. Vows are promises made for life and made in a spiritual context. For example, I promise to call you later, or I promise to do my best. But two partners vow to be true to each other throughout their married life, or I vow to be a brother for the rest of my life.

Vows are made in the presence of a community. They are a public profession witnessed by many people. Just as a couple who are saying their marriage vows do so in the context of a celebration with family and friends, a brother professes his vows in a similar setting.

*Vows are made in the
presence of a community.*

Poverty, chastity, and obedience are heavy words. They are, in a way, old-fashioned terms that seem almost out of place in twenty-first-century American culture. You don't hear them too often on commercials or see them printed on glossy magazine covers. They are words that people can easily dismiss as irrelevant and outdated. After all, who wants to be poor? Isn't obedience for pets? What does chastity mean, anyway?

Poverty

Let's start with poverty, which is a somewhat confusing concept. In Luke's Gospel, Jesus says, "Blessed are you who are poor, for yours is the kingdom of heaven" (6:20). But if it is a blessing to be poor, why does the nation spend so much time, money, and energy trying to get rid of poverty?

Perhaps *simplicity* is the word to use. This is the goal, after all. How can you live more simply, especially in the midst of a culture that is doing its best to convince you that you always need more? The words *new* and *improved* are the two most common descriptors in advertising. Look at how quickly a computer becomes outdated, a car depreciates in value, or clothes become unfashionable. It is a struggle just to keep up.

Although some brothers live with very little and in extremely poor areas of the world, the vast majority seem to have a pretty good life. They have their basic needs taken care of, are well educated, and live in a comfortable residence. For me it comes down to the issue of how I handle the money I earn.

The money the brothers earn is not their own but belongs to the community.

Other congregations of brothers may operate differently from a financial standpoint, but let me share how my Midwest District handles money. Brothers who draw a salary for their work—which is true for most brothers in active ministry—receive a paycheck made out to the brothers' community rather than to the individual brother. The money the brothers earn is not their own but belongs to the community. So, they turn in the check to their local community, which deposits it into an account.

At the beginning of each school year, when the brothers determine their Community Annual Program (CAP), they discuss the budget, among other things. The community—like any household—must budget its income and expenses. A significant portion of the budget goes toward paying the tax to the district. Although the De La Salle Christian Brothers, like all religious congregations, are tax exempt with respect to the government, they do pay taxes to the district to fund ministries, graduate study, novitiate, housing, retirement, health needs, administrative expenses, and so on. The district guarantees each brother an annual stipend through his local community. Most communities allocate a monthly amount for each brother's personal use.

Exceptions to this policy are the brothers who are working in mission areas where the local school or other ministry cannot afford to pay for their services. Some recent educational initiatives in the United States—for example, to serve people who are underprivileged—do not provide a salary to the brother but are instead subsidized by the district.

The bottom line is this: a brother's money is not his own; it belongs to the community. This is not to say that he has no personal money at his disposal. Like most people, brothers have to live within their means. I like going to movies, for instance, and I like to have popcorn during them, so I try to hit matinees whenever possible. This helps my monthly stipend last a bit longer. Generally, brothers use their stipend to purchase personal items, including toiletries, clothing, and cards and gifts for friends and family. Purchases such as groceries and household supplies, which benefit the whole community, are not counted as personal items.

The goal is to try to live simply and to realize that it is easy for money to control me rather than the other way around. In this sense the brothers' community life is countercultural. Today's money-driven culture insists that I need to make more and more money to get all the things it says I must have. The pursuit never ends.

At times I am down to a dollar or two by the end of the month, a situation not much different than that of millions of Americans. The big difference is that I have a community to support me. I will not get evicted at the end of the month for not paying the rent.

The constant challenge for individual brothers and particularly for their local community is to witness to a simple, shared life. Some houses and congregations are better at this than others. Witness is not easy. Take the simple fact that in my district brothers live together in community but do not work in the same ministry, so it is not practical to share one or perhaps even two cars.

It all comes down to a simple but continually challenging question: How much is *enough?* This is a question for brothers to ponder as a group and as individuals. As the saying goes, "I will live simply so others may simply live."

What do I really need? How do I draw the line between wants and needs? I will never forget the words of a young man who was hosting a group during a mission service trip to Tijuana, Mexico. I had accompanied some college students who were spending their spring break there. He explained that whenever he receives a new shirt as a gift or buys one, he gets rid of two old ones. His clothing collection stays minimal. He has what he needs rather than a closet full of clothes he seldom wears.

It is not easy in contemporary America to live simply.

His comment had an impact on me. Since then I have tried to avoid impulse buying. Do I really need this item, or am I getting it because I like it? Such questions keep me honest and focused on trying to live simply. I have the hardest time with books and music because I like both a lot. I do try to find the lowest price I can, which helps. It is not easy in contemporary America to live simply.

A brother's needs will always be taken care of. It is the wants that are the challenge!

Chastity

This word sounds so old-fashioned, doesn't it? For a lot of people, it means "not having sex"—but this limited understanding robs the word of its beauty and significance. Yes, it is true that a brother's vow of chastity means that he will remain celibate; he will not engage in sexual intercourse. But chastity means more than just not having sex. The fact is that all Christians are called to live a chaste life. You and I are called by our faith to live out our sexuality as the gift from God that it is. For married persons, chastity means sexual intercourse only with the spouse; for everyone else it means not having sexual intercourse.

This moral ideal does not mean that you and I are not sexual people. You cannot separate out your sexuality any more than you can separate out your emotions or your faith. Everything is blended within you to make you a unique person. If you try to separate out certain parts of your identity, you do damage to who you are.

Every part affects every other part. For instance, no matter what you are doing, when you see a particularly attractive person walking by, it is very hard not to notice. You can't help it. It's similar to when you walk into a room and smell freshly baked bread or chocolate chip cookies: your attention is immediately drawn to whatever smells so good.

Sexuality is a great, powerful, and often confusing gift from God, but it is a gift. We brothers live as celibate men because we have vowed to live a life of community and to refrain from loving any one person exclusively so that we can better love many people. The freedom of our commitment means that we are able to be more available.

The celibate life is a mystery in a lot of ways.

Relationships are essential for everyone. To grow as a human being, you need other people. A brother strives to develop relationships with others that are not sexual in nature but loving and freeing. The celibate life is a mystery in a lot of ways.

Just like anyone else—married or single, religious or lay, young or old—brothers need to reflect continually on the quality and quantity of their relationships. Brothers are called to be loving persons—persons who love the people God sends into their lives, especially young people, many of whom feel unloved and unworthy of love.

You and I live in a society obsessed with sex. It is easy to get the impression that everyone is having sex and that if you are not, something is wrong with you. This is a sad situation because sex, like so much else in today's society, has become a commodity used to sell products, to manipulate others, and to reduce a person to an object with a value based only on appearance.

Brothers are called to be witnesses to the fact that there is another way to approach sexuality and that it is possible to be healthy, loving men who have meaningful relationships that are not based on genital interaction. This is not to say that men who enter the community of brothers have not had sex. Virginity is not a requirement for entering a brothers' community, but celibacy is obligatory. In other words, a man who becomes a brother is expected to refrain from having sexual intercourse, no matter what his background or sexual orientation is.

I realize that out of all the aspects that make up a brother's life, celibacy is probably the biggest hurdle for anyone, especially a young person who is looking at this way of living the Christian life. My friends who are not Catholic find celibacy difficult to understand.

When I speak to student groups, this question invariably arises: "Can you get married?" Many young and not-so-young people cannot imagine not being married at some point. They certainly can't understand deliberately choosing celibacy over the joys of marriage and family.

I try to explain to them that living my life as a brother is incompatible with being married. It's not so much that I'm choosing celibacy but that I am choosing to be a brother, and being celibate is an integral part of that call.

All Christians are called to chastity.

Is it easy? Not always. But then neither is marriage or the single life. I have to make the choice over and over again because throughout my life I meet people I am attracted to. It is only natural, and it happens to everyone.

Another important thing to realize is that just because I am a celibate brother does not mean I do not have friendships with people who are not brothers. My closest friends are not brothers; several of my best friends are female. I cherish the friends in my life—both male and female—just as I cherish my family.

All of us need people in our life that we can confide in, trust, and just plain have fun with. Some of my friends are married; some are in relationships, and some are single. They are all special, and our friendship transcends the paths we have chosen for our lives. In fact, the different vocations make our friendship that much richer.

All Christians are called to chastity. For brothers, priests, and sisters, chastity means taking a vow of celibacy and knowing that loving others involves much more than sexual intercourse.

Obedience

You and I learned early on that we ought to obey our parents. We might not have been very good at it, but we knew that it was important. If you are a teacher, you expect—or at least hope—that your students will obey you. But to whom does an adult need to be obedient? Maybe to a boss or to a police officer. Or perhaps to God?

Think back to the Gospels and to how often Jesus would do something because it was his Father's will. He was simply obeying God, his Father. Aren't you and I called to do the same—to do the will of God?

The vow of obedience is a public acknowledgment of the fact that I am not really in control of my life. Oh, I think I am. I am even told that I should be, and in some ways this is good advice. No one else can make certain decisions for me about my health, my future, or my relationships. I need to make these decisions and live with the consequences. But in a larger sense, I know that much of what happens to me and within me is beyond my control.

When a brother takes a vow of obedience, he is saying, "I admit publicly that I am not entirely in charge of my life. I admit that a Higher Power is truly in charge. I need to listen to God working within me and around me."

Obedience is about *listening*. It is also about realizing that I alone do not make significant decisions about my life; I make them in the context of my community. In other words, the decisions are not just about me; I always need to acknowledge that I am part of something bigger.

Obedience is about listening.

For instance, when I am discerning a change in ministry, I begin talking it over with my community, my friends, my family, and especially with God. Where can I best serve? How can I best use my God-given talents and strengths?

Discernment is an area where I have been stretched and have grown a lot. Every new place I have gone to has involved a process of obedience. I have listened to what is going on inside of me, to what others are saying about what I might be good at, and to where the needs are. In the end I try to obey the call of the Spirit in my life as that call is mediated through other persons. In your life, as you listen, talk, and pray, where do you feel called?

Obedience is much more than just saying, "Yes, sir!" It is anything but blind. Obedience helps me to see more clearly and focus more sharply on where I am and where I am hoping to go. Maybe I can sum it up best by reminding you of what you hear your coaches and teachers say: "Now, listen up!"

The vows are designed to help my brothers and me get our priorities right. God is number one in our life; no other relationship is more important. Because of the example Jesus set for us, we strive to live simply; he called the poor *blessed*. The church invites us to pay special attention to the needs of poor people while we work to remove the conditions that contribute to poverty. We are called to love everyone who comes our way, to see the face of God in people, especially in young people and poor people. We are called not to obey our own will but to follow God's design expressed through the events and persons in our life and the stirring in our heart.

All Christians are called to poverty, chastity, and obedience; brothers and other religious are summoned to profess these virtues publicly and to live them intensely and with integrity. All that being said, living the vows is a constant challenge. The "big three" help keep brothers on the path toward God, the only path worth following and worth giving my life for.

Chapter 4

Teaching and Ministering

Touching Hearts

To touch the hearts of your students and to inspire them with the Christian Spirit is the greatest miracle you can perform. (*Meditations by John Baptist de La Salle*, no. 139.3)

Of all the writings I know of Saint John Baptist de La Salle, the Founder of the Brothers of the Christian Schools, this is easily my favorite. It goes right to what being a brother is all about, for me at least. Brothers are in the business of "touching hearts," which implies a special relationship between a brother and the students he teaches. It is not enough to be a good teacher. It is not enough to be well prepared in the classroom. It is not enough to have the respect of your students. No, brothers are obliged to forge a relationship with their students and to strive to inspire them. *Inspire* is a great word; you can almost see the two words: *in spirit*. Brothers are called to touch their students spiritually.

The title *Brother* implies a special relationship, a fraternal relationship. In an ideal world, a big brother is someone who watches out for you, cares about you, and lets you know when you've done something wrong. An element of "tough love" is part of being a big brother. In the day-to-day struggles in the classroom and in the school halls, a brother is encouraged to remember always that he is in the holy presence of God and to remind his students of the same.

The title Brother *implies*
a special relationship,
a fraternal relationship.

The students I have taught and am teaching now are gifts in my life. They may not always seem to be gifts, but they call out the best in me, and I owe them my concern, my attention, and my energy.

Being Available in Times of Crisis

For seven years, I worked at Saint Mary's University in Winona, Minnesota, with other brothers and Lasallian colleagues. I served as campus minister, and I lived in a freshman hall as a staff member in residence. This position gave me an opportunity to get to know first-year students in a setting outside the classroom and the campus ministry office.

I learned to know quite well a student who lived next to me, Steve; we would often chat out in the hall, plus we both sang in the liturgical choir. One day in my office, I received a call from Steve's mom; she was very upset. His grandfather had passed away, and the family wanted to let him know, but they couldn't bring themselves to do it over the phone. They asked me if I would break the news to Steve. A swirl of emotions engulfed me: I was honored and humbled, but I also knew it would be very difficult to do.

Steve was the oldest in his family and the only one gone from home, so now I was being called to be his older brother and break the news to him about the death of his grandfather, with whom he had a special relationship. I agreed to help, of course. Hearing the news was very hard on Steve, and he broke down. We talked for a bit, and then he called home from my office phone. I was glad that I could be there to help him through the initial shock.

A similar situation occurred a few years later, but a strange coincidence that day convinced me that grace was at work. Brent had graduated from Saint Mary's University a few years earlier, and because he had acquired a job in Winona, I would occasionally see him around town.

One January evening—it was a Tuesday, I remember, because it was two-for-one night at a local burger place—the brothers in my community had decided to go out and take advantage of the deal. That is where I ran into Brent and his girlfriend, and we chatted for a bit. I hadn't seen him for almost a year.

That same night, about nine o'clock, I received a phone call from his mother. She had no idea I had seen Brent just a few hours earlier, but she called to tell me that her husband, Brent's father, had died suddenly of a heart attack. She could not bear to tell Brent over the phone, especially because the death was so unexpected. She had no idea when I had last seen Brent, but she knew that we were in touch occasionally; she wondered if I would be willing to go over to his place to break the news.

*Being available
is what a brother's life is all about.*

What amazed me—and this is what I shared with Brent's mom—is that because I had seen him a few hours earlier, to call him would seem rather natural. The hardest thing is that I could not tell Brent why I wanted to see him, but I did tell him there was something I wanted to ask him in person, based on what we had talked about earlier that evening. This was a white lie, of course, but I had promised his mom that I would tell Brent the news only in his presence.

I drove over to his apartment and told him the sad news, which was difficult to do. After a few minutes, Brent called his mother and spoke with her. It was a draining evening as we talked afterward, and then his girlfriend came over. When I returned home late that night, I thanked God that I had been available to help Brent and his mom.

Being available is what a brother's life is all about. I read once that it is not so much your ability or inability but your *availability* that can make a difference in the life of others. As a brother, I am available and can help out in ways that people with family obligations might not be able to do. Students have confided in me many times in my career as a brother, teacher, and campus minister. Sometimes the information or the situation is such that I need to refer them to a professional counselor or a doctor for help. But I am glad and thankful to be the intermediary. You can't spell *brothers* without spelling *others*, right?

The earlier story about Steve has a humorous postscript. When Steve was a senior, he was a member of a campus fraternity dedicated to music. Because I sang in the liturgical choir and enjoyed music a lot, the members of his fraternity had decided to ask me if I wanted to join. I could, of course, forego the usual pledge period. The invitation was an honor for me, but the humor was in the way Steve asked the question. He sat down, and after some small talk, he asked me whether I would like to become a brother.

I remember looking at him curiously and wondering what he meant. What did he think I was? He looked at me, realizing that I was not comprehending his question. He rephrased it and told me that the fraternity had discussed it and wondered if I wanted to become a member. Then I understood. "But, Steve," I said, "I *am* a brother!"

"Oh, I know, but I mean a brother of Phi Mu Alpha. Once you're a member of this fraternity, it's for life."

"Steve, let me tell you; I know all about being a brother for life."

We both smiled. For various reasons I decided not to accept the kind invitation to join the fraternity. It would have been too awkward to be a brother twice!

Why Not Priesthood?

One question brothers get asked often is this: "What is the difference between a brother and a priest?" The question is understandable and a source of confusion for young people, many of whom have never encountered a brother before. I do get called Father Larry fairly often. Although brothers and priests in the Catholic church may seem a lot alike, there are some important differences.

Brotherhood and priesthood are two distinct religious vocations. Most people understand more clearly the role and ministry of priests; they are the sacramental ministers in the church. Only an ordained priest is able to preside at the liturgy of the Eucharist or, in more familiar language, to say Mass. This is the core of priestly ministry, and the Eucharist is the essence of what it means to be Catholic. Priesthood is an essential ministry in the church and a very visible and familiar one.

Simply put, brothers cannot say Mass. They are not ordained. They take vows, which means they are consecrated to God in a special way, but this consecration does not involve ordination. Many male religious orders do include both brothers and priests, but the distinction between them with regard to ordination is clear.

I do not feel called to be a priest. My call involves living in community and working with young people in an educational setting. Although I enjoy participating in the Eucharist, I have no desire to be the presider, or main celebrant. Brotherhood and priesthood are wonderful vocations, but each one has a specific focus. I have great respect for the vocation of priesthood, but I prefer to be a brother and to be called Brother, which describes how I see myself and how I would like others to see me.

Giants and Heroes

A French priest who died in 1719, a brother from Ecuador who died in 1910, and a brother from Wisconsin who died in 1982—these three men are my heroes. All three are now enshrined in the chapel of the De La Salle Christian Brothers in Rome. These giants among the brothers have had a deep impact on my life.

The French priest is Saint John Baptist de La Salle, the Founder of the institute to which I belong. The brother from Ecuador is Saint Miguel Febres Cordero, better known as San Miguel. The brother from Wisconsin is Br. James Miller, who was murdered in Guatemala in 1982 by a masked gunman.

It's amazing what a person of
faith and vision can accomplish.

Saint John Baptist de La Salle saw a need in his day and did something about it. He formed around him a dedicated group of teachers to work with the children wandering the streets while their parents worked to make ends meet. These teachers later became the first Catholic men's religious institute composed only of laymen. De La Salle revolutionized the educational system of his day. His legacy lives on in nine hundred Lasallian educational establishments in eighty countries.

It's amazing what a person of faith and vision can accomplish. Not that there weren't struggles and obstacles; there were lots of them. At the end of his days, Saint de La Salle said that if he had known what his life would involve, he doubts he would have taken the first step. Don't ever forget that saints have doubts and struggles too, but they eventually come to the point of saying what De La Salle did on his deathbed: "I adore in all things God's working in my life."

Putting yourself in God's hands will take you places you've never dreamed of!

Canonized in 1900, Saint John Baptist de La Salle in 1950 was proclaimed Patron of Teachers by Pope Pius XII. I have visited Saint Peter's Basilica in Rome several times, and I love gazing at the upper level on the right front side of the huge interior and seeing De La Salle up there with other great saints of the church. He is the only saint portrayed with a child, for he lived his life in the presence of young people. This honor is quite a legacy for a man who originally had no intention of doing anything other than being a successful priest in the wealthy cathedral district of his hometown. Putting yourself in God's hands will take you places you've never dreamed of!

San Miguel is the patron saint of Ecuador. I was a brother back in 1984 when Pope John Paul II canonized him. I was immediately attracted to this new Lasallian saint, noted as a great teacher, a skillful writer, and an internationally renowned scholar. He was the first native Ecuadoran to join the De La Salle Brothers. By the time he was eighteen, he was writing textbooks that the government of Ecuador soon adopted as official texts. Despite his many accomplishments, San Miguel always said that what he found most fulfilling was preparing his students to make their first Communion. Because the educational ministry where I currently serve is San Miguel Middle School, I feel a special attachment to this saint from Ecuador. He dearly loved ministering to young people; so do I.

One of my students moved from Ecuador with his family two years ago. When he visited the school and we talked about San Miguel, his family wondered whether this was the same San Miguel they know. As it turns out, they were from Cuenca, Ecuador, San Miguel's hometown. My student had gone to the school that evolved from the one where Brother Miguel once taught. Small world!

I met Br. James Miller only once, about two months before he died. He was on a home visit to central Wisconsin. I was teaching at his alma mater, where he first met the brothers during his high school years and then soon after joined them. I vividly recall Jim as he sat at the dinner table in the brothers' house and told stories about his experiences in Nicaragua and Guatemala, where he had spent almost all his life as a brother.

At that time—the early 1980s—Guatemala was experiencing a lot of turmoil and violence, and Jim knew he was in some danger because of his efforts to help poor people (a threat to those in power who preferred the poor to be weak). I remember that Jim said that despite the constant threat of violence, he had to go back. His hope was that if he were captured, he would not be tortured, as many political prisoners were; he did not think he could endure the pain. He said he would rather die quickly. Two months later, on 13 February 1982, while Jim was repairing an outside wall of the school in Huehuetenango, Guatemala, a masked assassin gunned him down. Jim died instantly.

Santiago (Saint James) Miller, as the Guatemalans called him, was much loved by the people he served. His legacy lives on in Casa Santiago Miller, the school that now bears his name. Last year, the brothers at the headquarters in Rome dedicated a memorial chapel to all the brothers who have been martyred through the years. When I saw the new stained-glass windows, I noticed that one of the figures enshrined in glass is Br. James Miller. I had never before known anyone who later ended up being commemorated in a stained-glass window. It seemed strange to see Jim up there, looking rather stiff and unnatural in the traditional robe of the De La Salle Brothers. Most of the brothers remember Jim in his green overalls and with his shirtsleeves rolled up; he was always ready and eager to get to work. Although the church has not formally declared him a saint, those of us who knew him hope that one day he will be canonized.

John, Miguel, and Jim—these are rather common names, but definitely not ordinary people. Each one was caught up in the Lasallian vision and made his mark in the world. Each one is a unique role model who points the way for his brothers. Every congregation of brothers can tell a similar story because each community has a history of heroes.

It is good to remind yourself sometimes that you have not gone through anything that one of the church's saints has not experienced in one way or another. It sure feels good to have friends in high places!

Back to the Basics of Serving the Poor

When I first began teaching, I always said to myself that a special place in heaven is reserved for middle school teachers. I couldn't imagine trying to teach early adolescents in the throes of puberty. I was a high school teacher and felt comfortable in that world. So what am I doing these days? Teaching and leading a middle school! God truly is full of surprises.

This phase of my life as a brother began in 1995. That fall, a small school named after San Miguel opened on the south side of Chicago with a sixth-grade class. One of my novitiate classmates, along with another brother and a married couple, started this new school in a violent and gang-infested neighborhood.

I was doing university campus ministry at the time, and I initiated student weekend service trips to San Miguel that year. The next summer, I spent about two weeks helping out with San Miguel's summer school. Soon the connection between San Miguel School in Chicago and Saint Mary's University in Winona grew stronger. I watched in admiration as I saw the effect this little school was having on the neighborhood, its students, and especially the staff and volunteers.

San Miguel School was a significant step for the Midwest District: the first new school opened in many years and the first Lasallian middle school in the Midwest. Most important of all, the school only charged as much tuition as a family could afford, which meant that only a small amount of the funds needed to run this school would come from tuition income.

This was clearly a step *backward* for the district! I say backward because we brothers were going *back* to our Founder's original idea of gratuitous, that is, tuition-free, elementary schools designed to educate the young children of the working class and poor people. San Miguel School of Chicago has touched the heart of everyone who has been a part of it, including me.

I knew it was time to move on: I just wasn't sure where.

During my seventh year at Saint Mary's University, I was discerning where I was being called next. As much as I loved campus life and working with college-age students, I knew it was time to move on: I just was not sure where. I prayed about it, and soon the answer became obvious. Why not open a San Miguel school in Minneapolis?

When a brother mentioned to me the growing Latino presence in the Twin Cities, I began exploring the possibilities. I found myself talking and thinking about the project more and more. Friends I spoke with commented about how excited I would get when discussing a possible San Miguel school in Minneapolis.

After a couple of months, two recent graduates of Saint Mary's University—young people whom I admired because they were so service oriented—decided that they too wanted to be part of this project. One of them was giving up a successful career as an accountant; the other, a good position at a thriving Lasallian high school. Suddenly this project was no longer *mine* but *ours,* and therefore truly Lasallian.

Bringing San Miguel Middle School of Minneapolis to birth has involved many struggles and challenges. Moreover, it has generated tremendous energy, enthusiasm, and support from many people. The school opened its doors in September 2000, staffed by two brothers, two volunteers, and a married woman who signed on as the ESL (English as a Second Language) specialist. Four people made the commitment to live in the neighborhood served by the school, an area some people are nervous about being in and driving through. For me it is now home, and the dream of San Miguel Middle School of Minneapolis has become a reality.

This experience has been a powerful and at times painful step forward in my life as a brother. I am dealing with young people who were not having success in their previous school. They need extra attention in a small, nurturing environment. Some days are very hard, and sometimes I long for the comforts and predictability of university campus life. I know that what my colleagues and I are doing is Lasallian to the core, and I cannot help but see Saint de La Salle smiling on our efforts. Here is yet another manifestation of his inspiring and powerful vision.

One of my tasks at San Miguel is fund-raising. Because the school receives no public funding and the families pay only what they can afford, raising money to keep the little school operating is a constant challenge. I used to look at professional fund-raisers and development offices and wonder why anyone would want to do that for a living. Well, here I am, spending a significant amount of time doing that very thing. But you know what? The difference for me is that I have helped give birth to San Miguel Middle School, so near and dear to my heart. I love talking to others about it and telling its story.

It's all about *zeal*, a word you don't hear often but one well known to the followers of De La Salle. A former Superior General, Br. John Johnston, describes zeal as "impassioned eagerness." I like that. I do feel a passion about what I am doing and about the students my colleagues and I are serving. People respond to the San Miguel story; it makes sense to them. The realization that few question its need or desirability is affirming and gratifying.

As I struggle some days in the classroom in ways that I have never experienced before, I hope that my early instincts were right: that God does indeed have a special place in heaven for middle school teachers!

Chapter 7

Other Brothers

Xaverians. Alexians. Marists. Jesuits. Franciscans. Crosiers. Oblates. Servites. No, these are not the names of sports teams or visitors from another planet. They are a sample of the many different congregations that include brothers or have only brothers in them.

Although I am writing about my experiences as a De La Salle Christian Brother, you should note the great variety of brothers' congregations. They fall into two main categories, brothers in lay congregations and those in clerical congregations. In other words, there are brothers in orders made up of only brothers and brothers who are members of orders that also contain ordained priests.

The institute to which I belong has no ordained members; all are vowed religious brothers. Several other brothers' congregations focus primarily or exclusively on education. Examples include Brothers of Christian Instruction, Congregation of Christian Brothers, Brothers of the Congregation of Holy Cross, The Marist Brothers, and Brothers of Saint Francis Xavier. These institutes sponsor and staff primary, middle, and high schools as well as colleges and universities throughout the United States.

Other orders of vowed brothers have a variety of ministries. Alexian Brothers focus primarily on health care. Brothers of the Sacred Heart emphasize youth-related ministry. Presentation Brothers are engaged in retreat work, social work, pastoral ministry, and youth ministry. Franciscan Brothers of Peace provide sanctuary for survivors of torture, maintain a food shelf for poor people, and visit prisoners and sick people. No matter what the ministry, the unifying features of brothers' congregations are their emphasis on shared community life and their outreach to people in need.

Many clerical orders include both brothers and priests. All are vowed members of religious life, but priests in these congregations tend to be involved primarily in parish and sacramental ministry. Although brothers are not ordained, they do a variety of tasks depending on their talents and abilities.

Many religious institutes of brothers and priests prefer to have their members be called by their congregational name rather than by distinguishing between priests and brothers. Examples include the Marianists: if you are a Marianist, this is how you identify yourself. Benedictines are all monks, whether ordained or not. Franciscans are all friars (another word for brothers) first, priests or brothers second.

Habits (like brothers) come in a variety of colors, shapes, and sizes.

One rather interesting and colorful facet of belonging to a specific congregation is the *habit*, the clothing worn by its members. Habits (like brothers) come in a variety of colors, shapes, and sizes. The Franciscan habit is quite familiar to many people: the long, brown, hooded robe with the white knotted cord around the waist. It is based on the robe that Saint Francis of Assisi wore when he gave up his inheritance and began his new life as a simple beggar. Dominicans wear a white habit; Benedictine monks wear a black one, and the Crosiers wear a combination of white and black. Each congregation's habit is rooted in its history and usually can be traced back to the founder of the order, as in the case of the Franciscans.

Saint John Baptist de La Salle designed a distinctive habit for the Brothers of the Christian Schools because they represented a new group within the Catholic church: nonordained men living in community and conducting schools but not belonging to a monastery. The brothers originally dressed in a black robe with a white extended collar, a cape, and a wide-brimmed hat. The traditional habit, still worn by many brothers throughout the world, has evolved into a black cassock with a long white split collar that resembles a frequently seen depiction of the two tablets of the Ten Commandments.

Many De La Salle Brothers in the United States wear black pants and what they call the stock and collar, a black shirt with a white collar that is distinct from the Roman collar worn by priests. Sometimes worn with a black suit coat, this clothing is more practical than the traditional robe.

What you wear does not automatically make you a brother.

I do not wear the De La Salle Brothers' official clothing every day. On the one hand, I resisted for many years the idea of wearing any kind of distinguishing garb. I felt—and still do at times—that wearing distinctive religious clothing sets me apart from the people I serve; I'm not sure whether this separation is always good or healthy.

On the other hand, I do appreciate the power of symbols; religious clothing means that I am publicly witnessing to a distinctive way of living out the Christian call. Plus, as one brother who is also a good friend says, wearing the same thing every day helps keep life simple in a fashion-conscious world.

What you wear does not automatically make you a brother. The same holds true for priests and sisters. Clothing may help people identify you, but at times it can also create a barrier or be an obstacle. In times past, virtually every congregation required brothers to wear the habit of their order. Sisters were also obliged to wear a habit that included a veil. This practice is no longer true for many congregations. Men and women in religious life now dress however they and their community judge they need to.

I appreciate both the advantages and the disadvantages of distinctive religious clothing. Each congregation makes a decision about its preference. There are lots of ways to give sign value to religious life. If not with the official religious habit, then with crosses or pins that members of a congregation can wear.

I believe it is important to let others know, especially new people I encounter, that I am a brother, whether or not my clothing sets me apart. Many people have never met a brother before, and they have lots of questions about what this means and how I am different from a priest or a pastor. Their curiosity gives me another chance to witness to what it means to be a brother.

Being a brother in the Catholic church can lead you to a great variety of congregations and ministries.

Br. Hilary McGee is a Franciscan Brother of Peace, an order founded in 1982 in Saint Paul, Minnesota. He has this to say about his community of brothers:

What drew me to the order is the great Franciscan spirit of my brothers and the wonderful prayer life we have in our community. We have many avenues of outreach to meet the needs of the poor. We are a strong support team for one another.

Br. Timothy Tomczak is a member of the Crosier Fathers and Brothers, founded in 1210 in Belgium. A brother in a congregation that is made up of both ordained and nonordained members, he speaks about the blessings and the challenges:

> The diversity of ministries makes life interesting. I like the sharing by ordained members of what is going on in their sacramental ministry in the church; however, the parish ministry seems at times to dominate our religious life. Being a clerical order means that we have to "fit in" with the church's structure, so brothers cannot be elected prior or provincial.

Brother Tim is referring to the stipulation in the rule and the customs of some clerical congregations that only ordained members can serve as the superior. This rule at times led to a sense of inequality between ordained and nonordained members, but most clerical congregations have emphasized the positive aspect that all members are called primarily to religious life; in this sense all are brothers first, whether ordained or not.

Br. Vincent Champine, a brother in the Dominican order, serves as assistant chancellor for the Archdiocese of Saint Paul and Minneapolis. He comments on the role of brothers in his congregation of brothers and priests:

> The role of brothers is to participate fully in the prayer life of the community and to develop their talents, education, abilities, and spiritual life. A brother's choice not to be ordained for a sacramental ministry leaves him free to pursue many ministries for which he is prepared.

Being a brother in the Catholic church can lead you to a great variety of congregations and ministries. Every congregation has its story to tell as well as its cast of characters, but whether you are a Christian Brother, a Franciscan friar, a Benedictine monk, or a member of any other order, a common theme unites all the members: you and they are brothers. As Psalm 133:1 exclaims, "How very good and pleasant it is when kindred live together in unity."

The Wisdom of Our Elders

I have been a De La Salle Brother for over twenty years, almost half of my life thus far, but in many ways I still feel just like a kid. Some men in my congregation have been brothers for over three times that long! Many of them joined when they were still in high school; they have lived through an incredible time of change in the world, in the church, and in religious life.

What it means to be a brother today is very different from what it was when my senior brothers joined. In the days before Vatican Council II, practically every moment and action of a brother's life was regulated—from the time he got up to the moment he went to bed. Brothers throughout the world followed the exact same schedule. The common saying was "Keep the Rule, and the Rule will keep you." The Rule is the manual, or guidebook, that every brother receives and tries to follow. What the saying meant is that following all the guidelines would make you a good brother.

This advice seems a bit too simplistic, and it does not allow for much personal freedom to make choices. Today's Rule in most congregations is very different and strives to be inspirational rather than only describing what a brother should and shouldn't do.

What is it like for the men who have devoted over fifty years of their life as brothers? What have they found most fulfilling? most challenging?

What has touched them about being a brother? Here are some comments and stories from the "old guys." Each brother, although officially retired, remains active and involved in some form of ministry.

Here are some comments and stories from the "old guys."

Br. Mark Gault is currently on the staff of Christian Brothers Retreat Center, near Stillwater, Minnesota. What has he found most fulfilling in his sixty-four years as a brother?

Seeing graduates and former students growing up to be good parents, members of their church, and effective workers—in other words, successful in their relations with others whether or not spectacularly fortunate in making money.

Brother Mark's biggest challenge has been "reaching students who are unwilling to give enough of themselves to be successful in a good way."

Br. Basil Rothweiler, a brother for sixty-six years, is now spearheading development efforts for the De La Salle Brothers in the Upper Midwest. His biggest challenge has been "teaching and administering in schools and religious communities through the pre– and post–Vatican II era, with all the changes in church and society." Brother Basil shares a special moment in his life:

It was a tonic for me to attend a golden jubilee celebration of a class I had taught as freshmen in a school in Texas over fifty years ago. The growth of the church and the city and the number of our graduates who gave leadership to this growth are amazing. This for me validates and gives dignity, value, and blessing to Catholic educators and Christian Brothers today.

Br. William Rhody recently began the Lasallian Tutors program, in which senior citizens spend time reading aloud to children. What he has found most fulfilling in his fifty-five years as a brother is "the willingness of the brothers to 'walk the talk.' Education is our mission. Brothers are encouraged to seek further education and degrees, and they are willing to change their focus in the mission when the times demand it." Brother William recalls a reunion with a former student:

My first year teaching was at Saint Mel High School in Chicago in 1949. After graduation that year, I lost contact with one particular young man I had taught. When I celebrated my silver jubilee twenty-five years later, he sought me out, and we have been friends through all these years. We stay in touch frequently.

Br. Theodore Drahmann, a brother for fifty-six years, is currently teaching at the Minneapolis campus of Saint Mary's University of Minnesota. He shares his biggest challenge as a brother:

It was to be a university president (at Christian Brothers University, Memphis, Tennessee). As I found out soon after assuming the position, I was called upon to be not only a specialist in and a spokesman for higher education but also an institutional administrator and financier, a beggar for outside support, a lobbyist with federal and state government, a corporation executive, a town mayor for the university, and even a sort of pastor as the religious leader of the campus. For thirteen years, with the help of my fellow Christian Brothers and many other wise and good people and with the grace of God, I was able to meet these challenges with some success.

Each of these four brothers, in the course of many years of service, has shared his talents and been stretched in different ways. One thing is true if you become a brother: invariably—sooner or later—you will discover talents and abilities you never knew you had! Often your own brothers will see something in you that you do not see for yourself. They will invite and encourage you to try new things and expand your horizons.

I can't think of a better way to end this chapter than to share Brother Theodore's reflection on his life as a brother:

When I boarded the train in the small town of Perham in northwestern Minnesota in September 1945, I was on my way to Missouri to begin my training as a Christian Brother. The son of a grocer, I had never been outside the state of Minnesota. I now look back with some astonishment to years of study and service as a brother in such diverse locations as Saint Louis, Chicago, Paris, Rome, Saint Paul, Memphis, and Washington, D.C. Instead of now being the retired grocer that I might have been, I am happy to continue to work with the training of Catholic school teachers, and I thank God for the remarkably wide experiences he has blessed me with during my life as a brother.

An Invitation to Dream

What's Next for the Brothers?

If being a brother is such a wonderful vocation, why are there so few brothers? This is a very good question; I wonder about it too.

The years after Vatican Council II saw a huge drop in the number of young persons entering religious life and the priesthood. The Council redefined religious life and encouraged every religious congregation to renew and update itself according to its original spirit. The result was that many brothers and sisters found themselves with much more freedom than they had enjoyed in the past.

Whereas in an earlier time, everyone followed a strict schedule that included everything from the exact moment to get up in the morning to required silent periods, now each local community in my institute sets its schedule for prayer and meals as an important part of the Community Annual Program. The Rule and the brothers' customs give much more attention these days to the realization that people have different rhythms and needs.

What it all boils down to is that my personal Lasallian spirituality, for example, is not imposed through conformity. Yes, the brothers pray together, but the role of individual prayer receives far more emphasis than in the past. Each brother needs to build his own relationship with Jesus. The community strengthens his spirituality and vocation, but ultimately it is up to each brother to find and follow his path to God.

A former student of mine used to walk into the campus ministry office daily and greet me by saying, "Hi, holy man!" At first, that sounded very strange to me, mainly because I knew I wasn't living up to the title. But as I got used to it, I grew to like it, partly because I knew that she meant it not only as a nickname but also as a sign of respect.

The greeting also highlighted the fact that I am seen, like it or not, as a committed religious man. I realize that the people I meet and the students I work with will form impressions of what brothers are like by their contact with me. I hope I make a positive impression, but I know this doesn't always happen.

Where are brothers headed? There are definitely fewer of us, and our median age is rising as fewer young men join our ranks. It is easy to despair and conclude that this lifestyle no longer appeals to young people. Perhaps some congregations have resigned themselves to the fact . that they will die out one of these years. (One joke is that the last one out should turn off the lights.)

Young people today want to make a difference.

Well, sorry, but I cannot believe that after three hundred years of touching the hearts of countless young people, the followers of De La Salle will fade away. Part of the challenge is to realize that far from becoming extinct, the Lasallian vocation is alive and well as more and more laypeople catch the spirit and make their own the dream and vision of Saint de La Salle. This new phenomenon is made possible in large part because there are fewer brothers to carry on the work. Other congregations of brothers are experiencing the same force and spirit among their colleagues and associates.

I also believe there is still a place for the vowed religious brother in this ever-expanding world of ministry. The challenge as brothers is to recapture the spirit of faith and zeal that impassioned the first brothers and so many who followed and opened schools throughout the world.

Young people today want to make a difference. They want to work in schools and in other ministries that are meeting critical needs, and to live in healthy, happy communities energized by prayer, kindness, and playfulness. So do I! Brothers need to keep reaching out and inviting young people to join them, especially young men with a dream in their heart.

Dreaming the Dream

Joan Chittister, OSB, a Benedictine, has written an inspiring and challenging book about religious life, *The Fire in These Ashes*. I close this chapter by quoting one of her sources and one of her reflections. First, she cites the Argentine author Jorge Luis Borges:

> Time is the substance I am made of. Time is a river which sweeps me along, but I am the river; it is a tiger which destroys me, but I am the tiger; it is a fire which consumes me, but I am the fire. ("A New Refutation of Time," in *Labyrinths*, p. 234)

Then Sister Joan adds her commentary on the passage:

> I am, in other words, what is to become. What is going on around me is going on within me now and will or will not happen because of me. I am both the vehicle and the substance of the future. What I am now, religious life will be in the future. There is no future without me because the future is within me. (*The Fire in These Ashes*, p. 37)

I love rivers, and I love being a brother. It works for me, even though at times I cannot explain why. It fits, and I know that wherever religious life and brothers in particular are headed, I am part of the river.

A dream is a powerful force.

God has planted a dream deep within you and me. Our task as faith-filled people is to uncover this dream and live it out. It may not be easy, but it is always life giving. The challenge is to stay open to the possibilities. As I've said before, brotherhood is my way to God. I know it is a big part of the dream God planted within me.

A dream is a powerful force. You cannot live out God's dream alone. At times it doesn't even seem possible that you can do it at all. Those are the times when it is good to remember the Holy Spirit's words to you through the letter written by Saint Paul (another dreamer) to the Ephesians:

Now to him who by the power at work within us is able to accomplish abundantly far more than all we can ask or imagine, to him be glory in the church and in Christ Jesus to all generations, forever and ever. (3:20)

"Far more than all we can ask or imagine"—those are inspiring words. Life is all about saying yes to a dream, and then, oh, the places you and I will go!

For Further Reading

Chittister, Joan, OSB. *The Fire in These Ashes: A Spirituality of Contemporary Religious Life*. Kansas City, MO: Sheed and Ward, 1995.

Palmer, Parker. *Let Your Life Speak*. San Francisco: Jossey-Bass, 2000.

Acknowledgments *(continued from page 4)*

The scriptural quotations contained herein are from the New Revised Standard Version of the Bible: Catholic Edition. Copyright © 1993 and 1989 by the Division of Christian Education of the National Council of the Churches of Christ in the United States of America. Used by permission. All rights reserved.

The quote on pages 9–10 is from *Evangelium Vitae*, by Pope John Paul II (Washington, DC: United States Catholic Conference, 1995), no. 61. Copyright © 1995 by the United States Catholic Conference.

The references on pages 24, 28, and 30 are from *Code of Canon Law: Latin-English Edition*, translation prepared under the auspices of the Canon Law Society of America (Washington, DC: Canon Law Society of America, 1983), nos. 648, 655, and 654, respectively. Copyright © 1983 by the Canon Law Society of America.

The quote on page 40 is from *Meditations by John Baptist de La Salle*, edited by Augustine Loes and Francis Huether (Landover, MD: Christian Brothers Conference, 1994), no. 139.3, p. 257. Copyright © 1994 by the Christian Brothers Conference. Reprinted with permission.

The first quote on page 63 is from "A New Refutation of Time," by Jorge Luis Borges, in *Labyrinths: Selected Stories and Other Writings*, edited by Donald A. Yates and James E. Irby (New York: New Directions, 1964), p. 234. Copyright © 1962, 1964 by New Directions Publishing Corporation. Reprinted with permission of New Directions Publishing Corporation and of Laurence Pollinger, Ltd.

The second quote on page 63 is from *The Fire in These Ashes: A Spirituality of Contemporary Religious Life*, by Joan Chittister, OSB (Kansas City, MO: Sheed and Ward, 1995), p. 37. Copyright © 1995 by Joan Chittister, OSB. Reprinted with permission.